CONNOR McDAVID

HOCKEY STAR

by Greg Bates

FOCUS READERS

WWW.FOCUSREADERS.COM

Focus Readers is distributed by North Star Editions:
sales@northstareditions.com | 888-417-0195

Produced for Focus Readers by Red Line Editorial.

Photographs ©: Curtis Comeau/Icon Sportswire/AP Images, cover, 1, 4–5; Jason Franson/ The Canadian Press/AP Images, 7, 18, 25, 27; Marcio Jose Sanchez/AP Images, 9; Jack Hanrahan/Erie Times-News/AP Images, 10–11; Jarid A. Barringer/Erie Times-News/AP Images, 13; Frank Gunn/The Canadian Press/AP Images, 15; Alan Diaz/AP Images, 16–17; Gene J. Puskar/AP Images, 21; Tony Gutierrez/AP Images, 22–23; Red Line Editorial, 29

ISBN
978-1-63517-868-5 (hardcover)
978-1-63517-969-9 (paperback)
978-1-64185-172-5 (ebook pdf)
978-1-64185-071-1 (hosted ebook)

Library of Congress Control Number: 2018931669

Printed in the United States of America
Mankato, MN
May, 2018

ABOUT THE AUTHOR

Greg Bates is a freelance sports journalist based in Green Bay, Wisconsin. He has covered the Green Bay Packers for nearly a decade. He has also written for outlets such as *USA Today Sports Weekly*, the Associated Press, and USA Hockey.

TABLE OF CONTENTS

CHAPTER 1

COMING THROUGH IN THE PLAYOFFS

Connor McDavid poked the puck away from a San Jose Sharks winger. In a flash, McDavid was off to the races. The Edmonton Oilers star is one of the fastest skaters in the National Hockey League (NHL). McDavid raced to the other end of the ice. He had only one defender to beat.

In 2017, McDavid (97) helped the Oilers win their first playoff series in more than a decade.

McDavid is known for his quick hands. And he used that quickness to his advantage. He unleashed a lightning-fast wrist shot around the Sharks defender. The puck flew between the goalie's legs and into the net. The hometown crowd went crazy. It was McDavid's first playoff goal, and it happened **shorthanded**.

The Oilers and Sharks were battling it out in the 2017 Stanley Cup playoffs. McDavid's goal helped lead the Oilers to victory in Game 2. The best-of-seven series was now tied at one game each.

Going into Game 6, the Oilers led the series three games to two. With one more victory, they would win the series.

The crowd goes nuts after McDavid scores a shorthanded goal.

The Oilers were up 2–1 as the clock ticked down in the third period. The Sharks took out their goalie so they would have an extra attacker. But McDavid had other ideas. From center ice, he flipped the puck into the empty net.

POSTSEASON EXPERIENCE

McDavid has always performed well in the postseason. Before he became a pro, he lit up the scoreboards for the Erie Otters. The **junior team** plays in the Ontario Hockey League (OHL). In the 2015 playoffs, McDavid scored 49 points in 20 games. That was third all-time in OHL history. The Otters lost in the championship round. But because of McDavid's incredible play, he was named the Most Valuable Player of the playoffs.

McDavid tacks on an empty-net goal in a playoff game against the Sharks.

McDavid's goal sealed the victory. The Oilers had won their first playoff series in more than a decade. And McDavid was a big reason why.

CHAPTER 2

BORN A HOCKEY PLAYER

Connor McDavid was born on January 13, 1997, in Richmond Hill, Ontario. He grew up in the nearby town of Newmarket, not far from Toronto. When Connor was just two years old, he got a pair of inline skates. His talent was clear immediately. It wasn't long before he started skating on the ice.

A young Connor McDavid looks for an open teammate during a 2012 junior game.

11

Connor's mother and grandmother often played goalie for him. But even when Connor was little, they couldn't stop his shots. By the time Connor was six, he was playing against nine-year-olds. And he **dominated**.

One day, Connor saw his dad and older brother working on hockey skills. Connor made up his own obstacle course so he could practice, too. He played hockey for hours in his parents' driveway. When it was too cold outside, he worked on his skills in the garage.

When Connor was 15 years old, he put up big numbers for the Toronto Marlboros. This team plays in the Greater

Connor fakes out a defender in a 2013 game with the Erie Otters.

Toronto Hockey League. Connor led his team to the league championship in 2012.

Connor knew it was time for a bigger challenge. However, he wasn't old enough to play in the top junior hockey league.

Most players don't start juniors until they are 16. But the league allowed Connor to play because he was so talented. Connor was the top pick in the league's **draft**. That meant he would be moving to Erie, Pennsylvania, to play for the Otters.

In his first season, Connor was named the league's Rookie of the Year. The next season, he won Most Valuable Player (MVP) honors. In his third and final season, he scored 44 goals and tallied 76 **assists**. His 120 points came in just 47 games.

Because Connor was so good, he was also selected to play at the **international** level. He won a gold medal with Team

Connor (17) competes with Team Canada in a game against Germany in the World Junior Championship.

Canada at the 2015 World Junior Championship. After a great career in the juniors, Connor was ready for the NHL.

CHAPTER 3

TOP DRAFT PICK

The Edmonton Oilers had the first overall pick in the 2015 NHL Entry Draft. And there was no doubt about who the team would select. Connor McDavid was the most NHL-ready player available. McDavid was in the crowd for the draft. When his name was announced, he stood up and hugged his parents.

McDavid admires his new Oilers jersey at the 2015 NHL Entry Draft.

McDavid leaves the locker room during his rookie season.

McDavid was excited to finally have an opportunity to play in the NHL. Growing up near Toronto, he had always cheered for the Maple Leafs. But he was happy to be playing for another Canadian team.

After all, the Oilers had a great tradition. The team was at its best in the 1980s when it had another young superstar. Most hockey fans agree that Wayne Gretzky was the greatest player of all time. And Gretzky led the Oilers to four Stanley Cup titles.

TWO YOUNG STARS

Growing up, McDavid was a huge fan of Pittsburgh Penguins star Sidney Crosby. Crosby wears No. 87 on his jersey. That's because he was born in 1987. McDavid borrowed the idea. He was born in 1997, so he wears No. 97. The two players have many other similarities. Both were the top overall draft pick. Both were great at a young age. And both have tremendous speed and skill.

McDavid hoped to become the Oilers star of a new generation. And he got off to a fast start. McDavid scored 5 goals in his first 12 games. Fans were excited to see where he might lead the team. But then he broke his left collarbone.

McDavid missed nearly half the season. When he came back in February, the Oilers were in need of a spark. McDavid brought it, finishing the year with 16 goals and 32 assists in just 45 games. However, the team still fell short of the playoffs.

Going into his second NHL season, McDavid was named the Oilers' captain. That honor is usually given to the best

Many hockey fans consider Crosby (87) and McDavid to be two of the best players in the game.

leader on the team. At just 19 years old, McDavid was the youngest captain in NHL history.

CHAPTER 4

MOST VALUABLE PLAYER

McDavid was healthy for his second year with the Oilers. And he quickly established himself as one of the league's best players. In the first 52 games, he had 17 goals and 42 assists. He led the NHL in scoring up to that point in the season. McDavid also scored the first **hat trick** of his career in November 2016.

McDavid celebrates the first hat trick of his NHL career.

When McDavid was little, he had scored three or more goals in plenty of games. But for a pro, it's a big accomplishment.

Because of his great season, McDavid was named to his first **All-Star Game**. In the skills competition before the game, he won the fastest skater contest.

Following the All-Star break, McDavid was just as good. He ended the 2016–17 season with an impressive 30 goals and 70 assists. No one in the league had more assists. And his 100 points made him tops in the NHL. For that, McDavid won the Art Ross Trophy. He also won the Hart Memorial Trophy. That award goes to the league's MVP.

McDavid battles for the puck in a 2018 matchup
against the Vancouver Canucks.

McDavid didn't have much time to celebrate his individual honors, though. He was preparing for his first trip to the playoffs. The Oilers won their first series against the San Jose Sharks. However, they came up short in the next round, with a tough loss to the Anaheim Ducks.

RARE COMPANY

When McDavid was named the league's MVP, he was only 20 years old. That made him the third-youngest winner ever. Penguins star Sidney Crosby and former Oilers great Wayne Gretzky both won the MVP award as teenagers. Gretzky scored 137 points in his rookie season. Crosby put up 120 points in his second NHL season.

Oilers fans toss their hats onto the ice during a 2017 game to celebrate McDavid's second career hat trick.

McDavid continued to play well, and he made his second All-Star Game in 2018. However, the Oilers had a disappointing season. But with McDavid leading the team for years to come, fans knew more trips to the playoffs were on the way.

CONNOR McDAVID

- Height: 6 feet 1 inch (185 cm)
- Weight: 198 pounds (90 kg)
- Birth date: January 13, 1997
- Birthplace: Richmond Hill, Ontario
- High school: McDowell High School (Erie, Pennsylvania)
- Junior team: Erie Otters (2012–2015)
- NHL team: Edmonton Oilers (2015–)
- Major awards: 2016–17 Hart Memorial Trophy (NHL MVP), 2016–17 Art Ross Trophy (NHL scoring leader)

Edmonton

Richmond Hill

Toronto

Erie

FOCUS ON
CONNOR McDAVID

Write your answers on a separate piece of paper.

1. Write a sentence that explains the main idea of Chapter 1.

2. In your opinion, what was McDavid's biggest achievement during the 2016–17 season? Why?

3. How many goals did McDavid score in his second NHL season?

> **A.** 30
> **B.** 70
> **C.** 100

4. Why didn't McDavid score many goals during his first NHL season?

> **A.** He was busy playing at the international level.
> **B.** He wasn't as good as other players in the league.
> **C.** He had a broken collarbone for half the season.

Answer key on page 32.

GLOSSARY

All-Star Game
A game in which the league's best players take part.

assists
Passes that lead directly to a teammate scoring a goal.

dominated
Showed that one player was clearly better than an opponent.

draft
A system that allows teams to acquire new players coming into a league.

hat trick
Three goals scored by one player in a game.

international
Having to do with many different countries.

junior team
A team for young players, usually between the ages of 16 and 20.

shorthanded
A situation in which one team has fewer players than the other, due to a penalty.

TO LEARN MORE

BOOKS

Butler, Erin. *Edmonton Oilers*. New York: AV2 by Weigl, 2015.

Hall, Brian. *Sidney Crosby: Hockey Star*. Mendota Heights, MN: Focus Readers, 2018.

Mortillaro, Nicole. *Connor McDavid*. North Mankato, MN: Capstone Press, 2016.

NOTE TO EDUCATORS

Visit **www.focusreaders.com** to find lesson plans, activities, links, and other resources related to this title.

INDEX

Answer Key: 1. Answers will vary; **2.** Answers will vary; **3.** A; **4.** C